AMAZING ANIMALS
OF THE WORLD ②

Volume 7

Nuthatch, Eurasian — Razor, Pod

GROLIER

First published 2005 by Grolier, an imprint of Scholastic Library Publishing

For information address the publisher: Grolier, Scholastic Library Publishing
90 Old Sherman Turnpike
Danbury, CT 06816

Set ISBN: 0-7172-6112-3; Volume ISBN: 0-7172-6119-0

Printed and bound in the U.S.A.

Library of Congress Cataloging-in-Publications Data:
Amazing animals of the world 2.
p.cm.
Includes indexes.
Contents: v. 1. Adder—Buffalo, Water -- v. 2. Bunting, Corn—Cricket, Bush -- v. 3. Cricket, European Mole—Frog, Agile -- v. 4. Frog, Burrowing Tree—Guenon, Moustached -- v. 5. Gull, Great Black-backed—Loach, Stone -- v. 6. Locust, Migratory—Newt, Crested -- v. 7. Nuthatch, Eurasian—Razor, Pod -- v. 8. Reedbuck, Mountain—Snake, Tentacled -- v. 9. Snakefly—Toad, Surinam -- v. 10. Tortoise, Gopher—Zebu.
ISBN 0-7172-6112-3 (set : alk. paper) -- ISBN 0-7172-6113-1 (v. 1 : alk. paper) -- ISBN 0-7172-6114-X (v. 2 : alk. paper) -- ISBN 0-7172-6115-8 (v. 3 : alk. paper) -- ISBN 0-7172-6116-6 (v. 4 : alk. paper) -- ISBN 0-7172-6117-4 (v. 5 : alk. paper) -- ISBN 0-7172-6118-2 (v. 6 : alk. paper) -- ISBN 0-7172-6119-0 (v. 7 : alk. paper) -- ISBN 0-7172-6120-4 (v. 8 : alk. paper) -- ISBN 0-7172-6121-2 (v. 9 : alk. paper) -- ISBN 0-7172-6122-0 (v. 10 : alk.paper)
1. Animals--Juvenile literature. I. Title: Amazing animals of the world two. II. Grolier (Firm)
QL49.A455 2005
590--dc22
                                                                                    2005040351

About This Set

Amazing Animals of the World 2 brings you pictures of 400 fascinating creatures and important information about how and where they live.

Each page shows just one species—individual type—of animal. They all fall into seven main categories or groups of animals (classes and phylums scientifically) that appear on each page as an icon or picture—amphibians, arthropods, birds, fish, mammals, other invertebrates, and reptiles. Short explanations of what these group names mean, and other terms used commonly in the set, appear on page 4 in the Glossary.

Scientists use all kinds of groupings to help them sort out the thousands of types of animals that exist today and once wandered here (extinct species). Kingdoms, classes, phylums, genus, and species are among the key words here that are also explained in the Glossary (page 4).

Where animals live is important to know as well. Each of the species in this set lives in a particular place in the world, which you can see outlined on the map on each page. And in those locales the animals tend to favor a particular habitat—an environment the animal finds suitable for life, with food, shelter, and safety from predators that might eat it. There they also find ways to coexist with other animals in the area that might eat somewhat different food, use different homes, and so on. Each of the main habitats is named on the page and given an icon/picture to help you envision it. The habitat names are further defined in the Glossary on page 4.

As well as being part of groups like species, animals fall into other categories that help us understand their lives or behavior. You will find these categories in the Glossary on page 4, where you will learn about carnivores, herbivores, and other types of animals.

And there is more information you might want about an animal—its size, diet, where it lives, and how it carries on its species—the way it creates its young. All these facts and more appear in the data boxes at the top of each page.

Finally, you should know that the set is arranged alphabetically by the most common name of the species. That puts most beetles, say, together in a group so you can compare them easily.

But some animals' names are not so common, and they don't appear near others like them. For instance, the chamois is a kind of goat or antelope. To find animals that are similar—or to locate any species—look in the index at the end of each book in the set (pages 45-48). It lists all animals by their various names (you will find the giant South American river turtle under turtle, giant South American river, and also under its other name—arrau). And you will find all birds, fish, and so on gathered under their broader groupings.

Similarly, smaller like groups appear in the set index as well—butterflies include swallowtails and blues, for example.

Table of Contents
Volume 7

Glossary

Amphibians—species usually born from eggs in water or wet places, which change (metamorphose) into a land animal. Frogs and salamanders are typical. They breathe through their skin mainly and have no scales.

Arctic and Antarctic—icy, cold, dry areas at the ends of the globe that lack trees but see small plants grown in thawed areas (tundra). Penguins and seals are common inhabitants.

Arthropods—animals with segmented bodies, hard outer skin, and jointed legs, such as spiders and crabs.

Birds—born from eggs, these creatures have wings and often can fly. Eagles, pigeons, and penguins are all birds, though penguins can't fly through the air.

Carnivores—they are animals that eat other animals. Many species do eat each other sometimes, and a few eat dead animals. Lions kill their prey and eat it, while vultures clean up dead bodies of animals.

Cities, Towns, and Farms—places where people live and have built or used the land and share it with many species. Sometimes these animals live in human homes or just nearby.

Class—part or division of a phylum.

Deserts—dry, often warm areas where animals often are more active on cooler nights or near water sources. Owls, scorpions, and jack rabbits are common in American deserts.

Endangered—some animals in this set are marked as endangered because it is possible they will become extinct soon.

Extinct—these species have died out altogether for whatever reason.

Family—part of an order.

Fish—water animals (aquatic) that typically are born from eggs and breathe through gills. Trout and eels are fish, though whales and dolphins are not (they are mammals).

Forests and Mountains—places where evergreen (coniferous) and leaf-shedding (deciduous) trees are common, or that rise in elevation to make cool, separate habitats. **Rainforests are different (see below).**

Fresh Water—lakes, rivers, and the like carry fresh water (unlike Oceans and Shores, where the water is salty). Fish and birds abound, as do insects, frogs, and mammals.

Genus—part of a family.

Grasslands—habitats with few trees and light rainfall. Grasslands often lie between forests and deserts, and they are home to birds, coyotes, antelope, and snakes, as well as many other kinds of animals.

Herbivores—these animals eat mainly plants. Typical are hoofed animals (ungulates) that are common on grasslands, such as antelope or deer. Domestic (nonwild) ones are cows and horses.

Hibernators—species that live in harsh areas with very cold winters slow down their functions then and sort of sleep through the hard times.

Kingdom—the largest division of species. Commonly there are understood to be five kingdoms: animals, plants, fungi, protists, and monerans.

Mammals—these creatures usually bear live young and feed them on milk from the mother. A few lay eggs (monotremes like the platypus) or nurse young in a pouch (marsupials like opossums and kangaroos).

Migrators—some species spend different seasons in different places, moving to where more food, warmth, or safety can be found. Birds often do this, sometimes over long distances, but others types of animals also move seasonally, including fish and mammals.

Oceans and Shores—seawater is salty, often deep, and huge. In it live many fish, invertebrates, and even some mammals, such as whales. On the shore birds and other creatures often gather.

Order—part of a class.

Other Invertebrates—animals that lack backbones or internal skeletons. Many, such as insects and shrimp, have hard outer coverings. Clams and worms are also invertebrates.

Phylum—part of a kingdom.

Rainforests—here huge trees grow among many other plants helped by the warm, wet environment. Thousands of species of animals also live in these rich habitats.

Reptiles—these species have scales, lungs to breathe, and lay eggs or give birth to live young. Dinosaurs are thought to have been reptiles, while today the class includes turtles, snakes, lizards, and crocodiles.

Scientific name—the genus and species name of a creature in Latin. For instance, Canis lupus is the wolf. Scientific names avoid the confusion possible with common names in any one language or across languages.

Species—a group of the same type of living thing. Part of an order.

Subspecies—a variant but quite similar part of a species.

Territorial—many animals mark out and defend a patch of ground as their home area. Birds and mammals may call quite small or quite large spots their territories.

Vertebrates—animals with backbones and skeletons under their skins

Eurasian Nuthatch
Sitta europaea

Length: 5½ inches
Number of Eggs: 4 to 6
Home: Europe, northern Asia, and northern Africa

Diet: seeds, nuts, and insects
Order: Perching birds
Family: Nuthatches

 Forests and Mountains

 Birds

© ROGER WILMSHURST / BRUCE COLEMAN INC.

The Eurasian nuthatch looks like a tiny woodpecker. It has a short bill as sharp and powerful as a chisel. Like many woodpeckers the nuthatch hammers at nuts. As it goes about its work, the nuthatch climbs in short, jerky steps. It can scramble along a tree trunk in any direction, even head-down. Unlike woodpeckers, however, the nuthatch does not need to use its tail as a prop. It can grip the bark using only its sharp claws and strong feet.

With its attractive blue jacket, the Eurasian nuthatch looks very much like its North American cousin, the red-breasted nuthatch, *Sitta canadensis*. The two species differ a little in size, the Eurasian variety being about an inch longer. Otherwise they are identical except for a slight difference in belly color. Within Europe the coloring of the nuthatch varies from place to place. The varieties in the south of Europe tend to have dark yellow breasts, while those in Scandinavia are almost white chested. Males and females look alike.

In addition to its bright appearance, the Eurasian nuthatch is loved for its cheerful song. Among its many tunes are a long, trilling "qui-qui-qui-qui"; a ringing, metallic "chwit, chwit, chwit"; and a forceful, repeated "tui!" Happily, this stubby little songbird is abundant in parks and backyard gardens. It appreciates a homemade nest box and is also fond of nesting in the walls of buildings.

Olingo
Bassaricyon gabbii

Length of the Body: 14 to 19 inches
Length of the Tail: 16 to 22 inches
Diet: fruits, insects, lizards, and small birds and mammals

Weight: up to 3½ pounds
Number of Young: 1
Home: Central and South America
Order: Carnivores
Family: Raccoons

 Rainforests

 Mammals

© MICHAEL & PATRICIA FOGDEN / MINDEN PICTURES

The olingo is a handsome, raccoonlike creature that lives in the rainforests of Central and South America. Its exotic name is derived from the Spanish word *oliente*, which means "foul-smelling"—the animal stinks like a rotting carcass. Just like a skunk, an olingo can empty its stink glands when attacked. A frightened olingo also screams with an eerie, piercing cry.

Despite its potent defenses, the olingo has many enemies. Its predators include ocelots, jaguarundis, owls, and boa constrictors. Fortunately for the olingo, it is fast and agile. With a little warning, it can easily escape danger by leaping and running from branch to branch. An olingo can jump up to 9 feet between trees. The only enemy that the olingo has not eluded is human. The creature is not hunted, but ranchers and farmers continue to destroy its rainforest home. In recent years the species has disappeared from many parts of Nicaragua, Costa Rica, and Panama.

Olingos are solitary animals, except for brief matings. They breed at any time during the year. After a pregnancy of about 75 days, the female gives birth to a single, helpless baby. The youngster nurses for about six weeks before starting to eat solid food. Descented olingos can be raised by humans in their natural habitat, but they do not thrive in captivity, largely because they are very nervous and timid.

Sea Orange
Tethya aurantium

Width: about 3 inches
Diet: plankton and dissolved organic matter
Method of Reproduction: cloning

Home: shallow waters of all oceans
Order: Tetraxonids
Family: Donatiid sponges

 Oceans and Shores

Other Invertebrates

The sea orange is true to its name both inside and out. In shape, color, and size, this sponge looks just like a bumpy, overripe orange. A cross section of the sea orange reveals a great similarity to the inside of any citrus fruit. White fibers called spicules divide the sea orange's inner body into wedges, much like the sections of a real orange. The creature even has a thick skin for a "peel." The sea orange's surface is dotted with pores through which it draws food and water into its body.

In their ocean-floor home, sea oranges commonly live on sandy or gravelly surfaces and in deep, rocky crevices. They can be found at depths of 300 to 1,000 feet below sea level, although some occasionally occur as deep as 1,300 feet. Mature sea oranges do not move on their own; instead, ocean currents roll them about for short distances. These animals reproduce by generating tiny buds called gemmules. Each bud contains a small mass of its parent's cells, protected by a hard coating. The tiny buds simply drop from the parent and float away. Eventually they settle to the ocean floor. When conditions are favorable, they mature into adults.

Sea oranges belong to a very ancient family of sponges. Their ancestors helped form gigantic ocean reefs in the Jurassic and Cretaceous oceans, when dinosaur-sized sea lizards ruled the watery world.

Great Gray Owl
Strix nebulosa

Length: 24 to 33 inches
Number of Eggs: 2 to 5
Home: Canada and
    northwestern United States

Diet: rodents and small birds
Order: Owls
Family: True owls

 Forests and Mountains

 Birds

© MARY ANN MCDONALD / CORBIS

The great gray owl is North America's largest. It is surprisingly unafraid of humans and often comes out during the day. Despite its boldness the great gray is seldom seen, because it has become quite rare. The owl has suffered from the destruction of its home. This dusky-gray owl is most comfortable in thick conifer forests and their surrounding meadows and bogs.

The great gray owl's favorite food is the vole, a small, burrowing rodent that comes out of its hole at night. Like most owls the great gray can find prey animals in the dark by following their tiny sounds. The bird's sensitive hearing is aided by the shape of its face. The curved disks of feathers around its eyes direct sound into the owl's ears.

The great gray owl has a special adaptation that allows it to fly silently. The front feather on each wing is rough. This ruffled edge allows the wing to softly cut through the air. As a result the owl can swoop down on its prey without warning.

During courtship, great gray owls give each other gifts of food. They also preen each other's feathers. Once she has laid her eggs, the female stays on the nest until her chicks are quite large. It is the father's job to bring food, first for the nesting mother and then for the entire family. The brood stays with their parents in the nest for several months, even after learning to fly.

Scops Owl
Otus scops

Length: 7½ to 8 inches
Weight: 3 to 4 ounces
Diet: insects
Number of Eggs: 4 to 6

Home: southern Eurasia and Africa
Order: Owls
Family: True owls

  Forests and Mountains

Birds

Summer Winter

© DIETMAR NILL / NATURE PICTURE LIBRARY

The small, slim scops owl is nearly impossible to spot as it roosts in the branches of shadowy trees. Its speckled feathers are perfect camouflage. In addition, scops owls in different regions can be found in slightly different colors, from grayish-brown to red, matching the trees in which they sleep during the day.

Europeans recognize the familiar scops owl by sound rather than sight. Its song is a sad one: a single whistling note repeated over and over again. The tone—a soft, clear "peeuw"—is one of the most familiar noises in the Mediterranean night. Sometimes it is mistaken for the croak of the midwife toad, which shares the owl's range in Western Europe.

A native of open woodlands, the scops owl has adapted to civilization. Today it is at home in parks, orchards, gardens, and town squares. It often flies around streetlights, where it catches large moths on the wing. This owl also eats crickets, cicadas, and other fat insects.

While most owls can survive a snowy winter, the dainty scops owl must leave for warmer places. Each fall, it migrates more than 2,000 miles to tropical Africa. When it returns north in spring, the tiny owl is ready to mate. It often nests in yards and along roadsides. The nest may be a tree hole lined with feathers or the abandoned nest of a songbird.

Short-eared Owl
Asio flammeus

Length: 13 to 17 inches
Diet: rodents, birds, and insects
Number of Eggs: 4 to 7

Home: North America, South America, Europe, and Asia
Order: Owls
Family: True owls

 Grasslands

 Birds

© HANS REINHARD / BRUCE COLEMAN INC.

Most owls are nocturnal—they sleep during the day and are active at night. The short-eared owl is unusual in that it is active during the day. As a result, it is one of the most familiar of the worlds' owls. However, this owl is growing rarer, especially in North America. For survival, it requires a country setting, where small prey animals are abundant. Sadly for the owl, rural areas are disappearing as cities and suburbs expand.

Short-eared owls eat mice, chipmunks, gophers, and other rodents. They don't bother to chew their prey, but swallow it whole. Bones and hair, which the owl cannot digest, get coughed up in little pellets about an hour after each meal.

In spring and early summer, short-eared owls mate in prairies, meadows, tundras, and marshes. As part of his courtship display, the male owl swoops over his chosen mate and claps his wings together beneath his body. After mating, the male and female scrape a nest in the ground, hidden among some tall grass or bushes.

Short-eared owl chicks do not hatch at the same time. The first to break through its egg has a great advantage in competing for its parents' attention. The last chick to hatch may get pushed aside at feeding time. In years when there is not enough food, this youngest chick may starve. But in years when rodents are abundant, short-eared owls can raise as many as 14 chicks!

Tawny Owl
Strix aluco

Length: about 18 inches
Weight: about 1 pound
Diet: small rodents, birds, and insects
Number of Eggs: 2 to 4

Home: Europe, Asia, and northern Africa
Order: Owls
Family: Owls

  Forests and Mountains

Birds

© ROGER TIDMAN / CORBIS

The haunting call of the "tawny," one of Europe's most common owls, can be heard in the dead of night, echoing through parks, large gardens, and established woodlands. The first part of its call is a deep, melodious "hoo-hoo-hoo," which is followed by a pause and a long, quivering "ooo-ooo-ooo-ooo." Although their call is familiar, tawny owls are rarely seen because they seldom hunt during the day. Someone lucky enough to catch a glimpse of the tawny owl will likely notice its enormous black eyes. Unlike Europe's short-eared and long-eared owls, this species has a perfectly rounded head with no ear tufts.

Most people appreciate the tawny owl because it devours such pests as house and field mice. The owl also catches sleepy songbirds, which it startles from their nighttime roosts. At dawn the owl retreats to its own roost, usually on a high, inside branch of a large, old tree.

Late March begins the breeding season. The female, which is slightly larger than her mate, usually nests in a large tree hole or in the abandoned nest of another large bird. Occasionally she makes her nest on the ground, sometimes in an old rabbit burrow. The female tends the eggs, but her mate diligently brings her food and helps feed the young. Tawny-owl chicks are ready to fly in about five weeks.

Red-legged Pademelon
Thylogale stigmatica

Length of the Body: up to 21 inches
Length of the Tail: up to 19 inches
Diet: leaves, fruits, ferns, and grasses

Weight: up to 15 pounds
Number of Young: usually 1
Home: eastern Australia
Order: Marsupials
Family: Kangaroos, wallabies, and wallaroos

 Rainforests

 Mammals

© KLAUS UHLENHUT / ANIMALS ANIMALS / EARTH SCENES

Pademelons are small reddish-brown wallabies that live in Australia. There are four types there: red-necked pademelons, red-bellied pademelons, Bruijn's pademelons, and red-legged pademelons. The latter live along the edges of the Australian rainforest and seldom step out of the confines of their sheltered areas. When frightened, they quickly run for cover in the rainforest undergrowth.

Red-legged pademelons usually live alone. But sometimes three or four gather around a particularly abundant supply of fallen fruits or a large bush ripe with berries. These animals are most active at dawn and twilight, but they also forage in the dead of night. Although common in parts of their habitat, the species is threatened by the continued logging of its home.

When a female is ready to mate, she emits a distinct odor. All males in the area are quickly alerted by the smell. They often fight over her, delivering powerful kicks while jumping in the air. Eventually the winner will mate with the female.

Scientists have not had the opportunity to fully study the habits of the red-legged pademelon in the wild. From what they know of related species, the researchers believe that the animal usually gives birth to a single, tiny baby. Blind and naked, the newborn must crawl from the mother's birth canal to her marsupial pouch, where it nurses and completes its development.

Rose-ringed Parakeet
Psittacula krameri

Length: up to 16 inches
Number of Eggs: 3 to 5
Home: native to central Africa and India; introduced elsewhere

Diet: fruits, berries, flowers, nectar, and seed crops
Order: Parrots
Family: Parrots

 Forests and Mountains

 Birds

© E. HANUMANTHA ROO / PHOTO RESEARCHERS

The bold, noisy rose-ringed parakeet is twice the size of a pet parakeet, or "budgie." Its call is a loud, rasping screech, and it is easily recognized by its bright red beak.

In the wild, rose-ringed parakeets tend to live in small flocks that feed harmlessly on fruits and flowers. But around farms and cities, these emerald-green parakeets gather by the hundreds. A large flock can quickly strip the seeds from an entire field of sunflowers or ruin an orchard full of ripe fruit. Rose-ringed parakeets will even rip open grain sacks in their unstoppable search for food. As a result, they are serious pests in parts of Africa and India.

As with most parrots, both sexes in this species are brilliantly colored. But only the male rose-ringed parakeet has the distinctive red collar around his neck. He is also distinguished by handsome black markings on his face.

Male and female rose-ringed parakeets perform a comical courtship ritual. The female begins with a dance, rolling her eyes and bobbing her head until a potential mate comes near. The two then rub bills as if kissing, and the male presents the female with a gift of food. After mating, the female lays her eggs in a tree hole or under a few loose roof tiles. She must incubate her eggs for a full three weeks, and the young parakeets do not leave the nest for nearly two months after hatching.

King Parrot
Alisterus scapularis

Length: about 16 inches
Weight: about 8 ounces
Diet: fruits, berries, and nectar
Number of Eggs: 3 to 6

Home: eastern Australia
Order: Parrots
Family: Parrots

 Rainforests

 Birds

© PAM GARDNER / FRANK LANE PICTURE AGENCY / CORBIS

The colorful king parrot spends most of the year in the warm, mountainous rainforests of eastern Australia. When the weather turns cold, the bird flies south to warmer lowland areas. King parrots are slow but powerful fliers that let out a loud, shrill call as they travel. The parrots' short winter migration frequently ends in farmlands and city suburbs. Unfortunately, hungry king parrots sometimes destroy valuable orchard crops and vegetable gardens. In the wild, they are content to feed on the fruit and nectar of acacia and eucalyptus trees.

In September, which is spring in Australia, king parrots return to the highlands to breed. The male courts a mate by puffing his feathers and flicking his wings. If the interest is mutual, the female responds by bobbing her head. Once mated, the pair remain together for life. Both sexes are colorful, but in different ways. The male's head and underparts are bright red, while the female's are green. He has a red bill and yellow eyes; she has a gray bill and white eyes.

Mated king parrots usually build their nest deep in a hollow tree trunk or in the branch of a dead eucalyptus. The female incubates the pure-white eggs for about 20 days. Although the male seldom enters the nest, he remains nearby to guard his mate. About five weeks after they hatch, the young parrots learn to fly. The family usually stays together until the end of the summer.

Kitten's Paw
Plicatula gibbosa

Length: 1 inch
Weight: ½ ounce
Home: Atlantic Ocean from North Carolina to the Caribbean Sea

Diet: algae and phytoplankton
Order: Oysters
Family: Scallops with bodies attached to shells

 Oceans and Shores

 Other Invertebrates

© PATTI MURRAY / ANIMALS ANIMALS / EARTH SCENES

The kitten's paw is a mollusk that is named for the shape of its lovely scalloped shell. Swimmers and divers often find large groups of kitten's paws clumped together along the edges of coral reefs. It is easier for the kitten's paw to reproduce in such crowded colonies. A change in water conditions, such as a rise in temperature, will trigger both male and female kitten's paws to release their sperm and eggs at the same time.

To keep itself from sinking into the sand and mud, the kitten's paw uses a fleshy foot that ends in a suction cup to attach itself to a shell or rock. Like other mussels, the kitten's paw needs to keep its "head" above the dirt in order to breathe and to catch its food. It draws water into its soft, meaty body through a funnel-shaped structure lined with tiny, waving hairs. The hairs push the water deeper and deeper inside. The kitten's paw's stomach then absorbs the oxygen dissolved in the water, as well as nutritious bits of algae and plankton.

Mussels such as the kitten's paw are important members of our global community, says Dr. Silvard Kool, a mollusk expert at Harvard University. "They keep our oceans clean by filtering out pollutants that we put into the water," he explains. Though we can depend on mussels to eat some of our pollution, we must then be careful not to eat the contaminated mussels. Shellfish living in polluted waters can be poisonous.

Galápagos Penguin
Spheniscus mendiculus

Height: 20 inches
Diet: fish and squid
Number of Eggs: 2

Home: Galápagos Islands
Order: Penguins
Family: Penguins

Oceans and Shores

Birds

Endangered Animals

© WOLFGANG KAEHLER / CORBIS

Penguins are supposed to live near the South Pole and frolic in the snow, right? Well, one species—the Galápagos penguin—is almost tropical. It lives close to the equator on the Galápagos Islands, 580 miles off the coast of Ecuador.

Penguins are able to survive near the equator because of a unique natural phenomenon. Although situated in the tropics, the Galápagos Islands are bathed in cold water by the Humboldt Current. This powerful stream wells up from deep in the frigid ocean and sweeps north toward Central America. The cold water keeps the local weather cool. In addition the current carries nutritious plankton. The plankton supply food for larger sea creatures such as fish and squid, which in turn are eaten by the Galápagos penguins.

The Galápagos penguin is the rarest penguin in the world. An endangered species, the bird is protected by law from hunting. But its small population remains in danger of being wiped out by natural causes. In 1982 and 1983, for example, a weather pattern called El Niño brought warm water and rainy weather to the Galápagos. As a result the plankton in the ocean disappeared, along with the fish and squid. The Galápagos penguins were then left without food for many months. Although the adult penguins were able to survive, they had no fish to bring their young. Weak and miserable, many penguin chicks died in the constant rain.

Gentoo Penguin
Pygoscelis papua

Length: 28 to 32 inches
Weight: 12 to 14 pounds
Diet: fish, squid, and krill
Number of Young: 2

Home: Antarctic Peninsula and
subantarctic islands
Order: Penguins
Family: Penguins

 Arctic and
Anarctic

 Birds

© PAUL A. SOUDERS / CORBIS

The gentoo penguin is a shy, rather timid creature. A gentoo sharing a beach with penguins of other species flees if the other birds behave in a bold manner. Among other gentoos, this penguin seems to go out of its way to avoid a fight. Even when defending their territories, male gentoos do little more than open their beaks and gape at one another.

What seems like cowardly behavior has helped preserve the gentoo penguin. Seal hunters who descended on the south polar islands in the past century killed many birds and took their eggs for food. The gentoo, of course, was off someplace else, hiding. By the time the sealing expeditions had ended, many of the friendly birds were extinct or endangered. With fewer other birds around, the gentoo, having avoided the slaughter, had more than enough food to eat.

No one knows for sure why the English-speaking residents of the Falkland Islands call this penguin "gentoo." Many theories have been put forth. The most logical of these suggests that this penguin's white "headband"—a feature peculiar to the gentoo—reminded the English settlers of an Indian turban. In the past the name "Gentoo" referred to a Hindu. Even more difficult to figure out is the origin of the seal hunters' nickname for the gentoo: Does anybody know why someone would call a penguin "Johnny"?

European Perch
Perca fluviatilis

Diet: small fish, insects, crawfish, worms, and other invertebrates
Number of Eggs: up to 200,000

Home: Eurasia
Length: 6 to 12 inches
Order: Perchlike fishes
Family: Perches and basses

 Fresh Water

 Fish

© HANS REINHARD / BRUCE COLEMAN INC.

European perch spawn from March through July. When she is ready to shed her eggs, the female glides over some stones or plants. She presses down her fins as her eggs squirt from her body in long, torn ribbons. A large, mature female can produce a string of up to 200,000 eggs. As soon as the eggs are laid, one or more brightly colored males fertilize them.

After 8 to 10 days, the young European perch hatch from their eggs. Each newborn perch immediately swims to the surface, where it fills its swim bladder with air. This bubble of air inside its body keeps the fish from sinking in the water. While they are young and small, European perch swim in schools. Together, they hunt insects and tiny freshwater crustaceans. As they mature, perch become less social, and as adults, they avoid each other except to mate.

Many people believe that the European perch and the North American yellow perch, *P. flavescens*, are one and the same species. Although they live half a world apart, both kinds of perch may share a common ancestor. Both species live in the same types of streams, ponds, and lakes. Their favorite haunts are the weedy edges near the banks of a pool or stream. Both European and North American perch are doing well, despite some problems with water pollution. In fact, the yellow perch's range is expanding as fishermen introduce it into nonnative rivers and lakes.

Southern Giant Petrel
Macronectes giganteus

Length: 34 to 39 inches
Wingspan: nearly 8 feet
Diet: fish and dead animals
Number of Eggs: 1

Home: southern oceans
Order: Tubenoses
Family: Shearwaters and petrels

Oceans and Shores

Birds

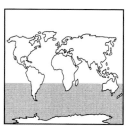

© THEO ALLOFS / CORBIS

Southern giant petrels are nicknamed "stinkers." Like all petrels, this species has a strong musky smell. The odor is made worse by the petrel's habit of feeding on dead animals. The bird often comes to shore to eat the decaying bodies of beached whales and dead seals. It rips into animal flesh with its sharp, massive bill. Giant petrels can inflict a nasty bite when bothered.

As its name suggests, the giant petrel is the largest of the 72 species in its family of ocean-dwelling birds. From wingtip to wingtip, the bird can grow to be wider than the average automobile! Giant petrels glide over the ocean, almost effortlessly, for days at a time. While most petrels are clumsy on land, the southern giant petrel walks quite easily.

Giant petrels breed on the Antarctic coast and on islands throughout the southern seas. The adults build a round nest of pebbles and dirt on a rock ledge or open ground. Their single white egg takes nearly two months to develop and hatch. The chick remains in the nest for several more months. It eats an energy-rich diet of marine oil, which its parents cough up from their stomachs. The adult petrels extract and store the oil from the seafood they eat. In addition to using the oil to feed their chicks, southern giant petrels use it as a weapon. When bothered, they spit mouthfuls of the stinky oil in the face of their enemies!

Reeve's Pheasant
Syrmaticus reevesii

Length: 20 to 35 inches
Weight: up to 3⅓ pounds
Diet: seeds, shoots, berries, insects, and small invertebrates

Number of Eggs: 7 to 15
Home: China and Japan
Order: Game birds
Family: Pheasants and quails

 Forests and Mountains

 Birds

© ERWIN & PEGGY BAUER / BRUCE COLEMAN INC.

The handsome Reeve's pheasant is native only to the hills and mountains of northern China. While most other pheasant live in grasslands and prairies, this species thrives in thickly wooded areas, where unlogged and undisturbed forests provide food in the thick leaf litter.

This is a typical pheasant, about the size of the familiar North American ring-necked pheasant. And like other pheasant, the cock (male) is larger and showier than the hen (female). Although the male's feathers are mainly buff-colored, they are handsomely edged in dark brown and black. The cock wears a distinctive black collar around his white neck and throat. His belly is entirely black, and his long tail sweeps the ground.

The female is a drab brown and sports a short tail.

When European hunters heard about this Chinese pheasant, they were very interested in bringing it to the New World. They wanted a hardy game bird that could survive in thick woods. Wealthy gentlemen imported a population of Reeve's pheasant to the Scottish Highlands in the 1800s. The pheasant survived for 30 or 40 years before dying out. Another group of pheasant, introduced in Austria in 1900, thrived until 1930, but they, too, eventually disappeared. Only in Japan, where the climate and vegetation are similar to China's, has this woodland pheasant been able to succeed in a new home.

Common Piddock
Pholas dactylus

Method of Reproduction: egg layer
Home: northeastern Atlantic Ocean and the Mediterranean Sea

Length: up to 6 inches
Diet: plankton
Order: Deep-burrowing and -boring clams
Family: Piddock clams

 Oceans and Shores

 Other Invertebrates

© JAMES KING-HOLMES / SPL / PHOTO RESEARCHERS

The common piddock burrows deeply into the sand on the floor of the Atlantic Ocean and the Mediterranean Sea. Using the sharp sides of its shell, it scrapes and bites the ground to make itself a chamber. The piddock also burrows in hard clay, wood, and even soft rocks. Hard ridges on the piddock's shell act like cutting teeth to help the clam dig. While the piddock grows, it must constantly enlarge its home. As it burrows, the clam turns around and around, nibbling away at all sides of its home.

Because its buries itself so deeply, the common piddock must have a very long feeding tube, or siphon. It extends its long siphon up out of its burrow and into the open water. Like other clams, the piddock sucks in water and filters out dissolved oxygen and floating bits of food.

When it's time to mate, male and female common piddock clams squirt their eggs and sperm into the water outside their burrows. The eggs and sperm mix quite haphazardly in the water currents. The fertilized eggs hatch into flealike creatures called "trochophores," whose bodies are rimmed with tiny hairs called "cilia." The trochophores swim by beating their cilia like oars. The young clams change shape several times before settling to the bottom of the ocean and digging a home. Common piddocks grow hard shells only as adults.

Giant Forest Pig
Hylochoerus meinertzhageni

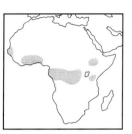

Length of the Body: 4 to 7 feet
Length of the Tail: 10 to 18 inches
Diet: grasses, herbs, leaves, fruits, dead animals, bird eggs, and insect larvae

Weight: 220 to 605 pounds
Number of Young: 2 to 4
Home: central Africa
Order: Even-toed hoofed mammals
Family: Pigs

 Forests and Mountains

 Mammals

© DAVID MADISON / BRUCE COLEMAN INC.

The giant forest pig is the largest pig in the world. It is also, arguably, one of the ugliest animals in the world. Even the homely warthog looks pretty in comparison!

Like the warthog, the giant forest pig has huge bumps under its eyes. These "warts" grow out of the animal's cheekbones and contain glands that secrete a foul-smelling liquid. The giant forest pig's bumps may protect the pig's eyes as the animal crashes through thorny forests. Male forest pigs, or boars, also have long yellow-stained fangs that curl up around their hairy snout. As for the forest pig's body…it is covered with scraggly, 6-inch-long bristles.

As if the giant forest pig were not ugly enough, it rolls in the mud and rubs against gooey spurge trees. The dried mud and sticky sap protect the pig's skin from insects and the sun. So hard is the pig's gunk-crusted hide that African natives sometimes use the leather as shields in battle.

Giant forest pigs live in families that trot through the forest each day in single file. Sometimes the boars fight to establish rank. They charge at each other head-on, colliding with a loud "whack!" The tremendous crash can crack a boar's skull and kill the animal. The winner of the battle announces his victory by spraying urine, drooling, and grinding his teeth. The loser usually runs away with his tail in the air.

Collared Pika (Alaskan Pika)
Ochotona alpina collaris

Length of the Body: about 7 inches
Weight: about 4 ounces
Diet: grasses, sedges, and other weeds

Number of Young: 2 to 6
Home: Alaska and the Yukon
Order: Lagomorphs
Family: Pikas

 Forests and Mountains

 Mammals

© MATTHIAS BREITER / MINDEN PICTURES

Although pikas resemble guinea pigs in appearance and size, they are most closely related to rabbits and hares. They are small, pudgy creatures with large ears and short, rounded legs and feet. Like a guinea pig, the pika has no visible tail. And like a rabbit, it jumps rather than runs.

There are two species of pika in North America. The collared, or Alaskan, pika differs littler from its southern cousin, the common, or North American, pika. The collared pika is distinguished by a pale-gray ring of fur on its neck and shoulders. Its body is brown across the back, gray on the sides, and whitish on the belly.

Pikas are known for their cheerful calls. The voice of the collared pika rings out during the day and into the early evening. The sound bounces off the steep hillsides and rocky mountains where it lives. The pika is often compared to a ventriloquist because it seems able to "throw" its voice so that the sound appears to come from somewhere else. To do this the pika jumps up and slightly forward with each call. The sound then echoes off the rocky cliffs in a manner that could confuse a predator.

In summer the collared pika gathers grasses and other green plants. Whatever it cannot eat on the spot, it spreads out on the rocks to dry in the sun. Then, like a farmer gathering hay, the pika stacks its dried food inside its den for the winter.

Water Pipit
Anthus spinoletta

Length: 6 to 7 inches
Number of Eggs: usually 4 to 6
Diet: insects and other invertebrates

Weight: less than 1 ounce
Home: Europe, Asia, and North America
Order: Perching birds
Family: Pipits and wagtails

 Fresh Water

Birds

© RAY TIPPER / LONELY PLANET IMAGES

The water pipit gets its peculiar name from the sound it makes. As it flies, it often calls "tsip-it," which also may sound like "pi-pit." This little bird is more often heard than seen. It is very small, about the size of a sparrow, but with a more slender bill. The water pipit can be found in a variety of habitats, including fields, marshes, meadows, seashores, and even the Arctic tundra! It spends most of its time on the ground, walking or running. A pipit presents a curious appearance as it walks: it constantly nods its head and wags its tail. This odd habit gave the water pipit its other name: the wagtail.

The water pipit enjoys a varied diet, eating all kinds of insects—including ants, grasshoppers, and beetles. It also will eat spiders, small mollusks and crustaceans, and seeds. It builds its nest on the ground using dried grasses, twigs, and moss. The nest is lined with soft fibers and animal hair. The female does most of the work, building the nest and incubating the eggs. Both parents care for the young birds until they are ready to leave the nest, about two weeks after hatching.

In North America, water pipits summer anywhere from the Arctic to as far south as the Rocky Mountains. They migrate in the fall, flying south in enormous flocks. They return north in March or early April, often stopping in their travels to feed in pastures and freshly plowed fields.

White Piranha
Serrasalmus rhombeus

Length: up to 12 inches
Method of Reproduction: egg layer
Home: Amazon River Basin of South America

Diet: usually small fish
Order: Carps and their relatives
Family: Characins

 Fresh Water

 Fish

© JANY SAUVANET / NHPA

White piranhas have a bad reputation—and for good reason! They are vicious fish that may bite anything that moves. White piranhas live in South America in the Amazon River and its tributaries, in groups called schools. A school quickly investigates any disturbance in the water, because noise often means the presence of a meal. The scent of blood in the water also attracts these fish.

White piranhas feed mainly on small fish, including other piranhas. But schools of these fish will viciously attack large animals, especially if the animals are bleeding. A pig can be reduced to a bare skeleton within minutes as a school of piranhas bite off pieces of the pig's flesh with their razor-sharp teeth. The teeth on a white piranha's lower jaw fit between those on the upper jaw. An animal caught in these "jaws of death" has no chance of escaping unharmed.

White piranhas have enemies, too. South American Indians catch the piranhas and eat their tasty flesh. Fishermen must use wire fishing lines to catch piranhas because the fish's teeth can easily cut through string and plastic. The Indians also use the white piranhas' teeth as scissors or razor blades. Some Indians even call ordinary scissors "piranhas"!

Spur-winged Plover
Hoplopterus spinosus

Length: about 10 inches
Wingspan: about 30 inches
Weight: about 5 ounces
Diet: insects, worms, and
   crustaceans

Number of Young: 3 to 5
Home: eastern Mediterranean,
   the Middle East, and Africa
Order: Water birds
Family: Plovers

  Fresh Water

Birds

The handsome spur-winged plover is unmistakable in its crisp suit of black, white, and brown. It is named for the sharp, slightly curved spur, or spine, on the front bend of each wing. When defending its territory from other plovers, the spurwing bats the intruder with one of its wings.

Spur-winged plovers are not social birds. Each mated pair typically lives in a separate territory along the shores of a marsh or lagoon. They nest in a small depression, which they peck and scrape in the ground. After the female lays her eggs, both parents take turns incubating them. As one sits on the nest, the other tosses dirt, twigs, and pebbles around it. This creates a sturdy, round wall around their otherwise simple

nest. On hot days the spur-winged plover wets its belly before settling down on the nest. This may help cool the eggs.

The eggs hatch a little more than three weeks after they are laid. The parents immediately lead their hatchlings out of the nest and down to the water. The chicks quickly learn to find their own food. But they stay near their parents for protection. When the parents cry in alarm, the young chicks instantly flatten themselves against the ground, while the older chicks run for cover. If a predator pursues the chicks, the parents attack, screaming and pecking. Neighboring plovers often join in a mob to chase the attacker away.

Red-crested Pochard
Netta rufina

Length: about 22 inches
Wingspan: about 34 inches
Weight: about 2½ pounds
Diet: mainly aquatic plants
Number of Eggs: 6 to 14

Home: Europe and Asia
Order: Ducks and screamers
Family: Swans, geese, and ducks

 Fresh Water

 Birds

© S. NIELSEN / BRUCE COLEMAN INC.

The red-crested pochard is a plump diving duck with a big head and big feet. It is best recognized by its head feathers. The male has a chestnut-red crown, while the female's is dark brown. When excited, they erect their head feathers into bushy crests.

These ducks live in the warmer regions of Central Asia and in isolated populations throughout Europe. They prefer weedy, reedy lakes with lots of open water. Occasionally flocks settle along protected beaches and seas. They are not particularly disturbed by civilization, but they keep their distance from people. The population of this pochard declined in Western Europe during the 19th century because of overhunting. Today populations are on the increase.

The red-crested pochard is most active during the day. It dives easily and deeply to lake bottoms, pulling up stems and roots. Just before it dives, the pochard makes a little leap into the air. It also flips upside down as it floats, eating plants near the surface. At night, most flocks roost in the center of a lake, although some rest on the shore.

In late spring the female builds a broad, bowl-shaped nest near the shore or on matted reeds in the water. At first the male guards his nesting mate. But he deserts her before the eggs hatch. The ducklings stay with their mother for about three months.

Striped Polecat (Zorilla)
Ictonyx striatus

Length of the Body: 11 to 16 inches
Length of the Tail: 8 to 12 inches
Weight: 15 to 50 ounces
Number of Young: 2 or 3

Diet: small rodents, birds, insects, snakes, and eggs
Home: sub-Saharan Africa
Order: Carnivores
Family: Weasels, badgers, skunks, and otters

 Grasslands

 Mammals

© MITCH REARDEN / LONELY PLANET IMAGES

The zorilla did not earn its Sudanese nickname, "the father of stink," for nothing! If it feels threatened, it emits a horrible-smelling spray from glands under its tail. In fact, the zorilla, with its thick black fur marked with broad white stripes and a long, bushy white tail, looks very much like an everyday American skunk. Like the skunk, the zorilla's distinctive markings warn other animals to stay away.

Zorillas live in a variety of habitats, from lowlands to high mountains, but never in dense forests. They sleep in burrows and rock crevices by day, prowling about at night for prey. Zorillas are good all-around athletes: although they usually hunt on the ground, they also can climb trees and swim well. Their main enemies are birds of prey and large carnivores.

People like zorillas because they prey on mice and rats. In fact, many people in Africa keep zorillas as pets. Although they do make good pets, their owners must be careful not to do anything to frighten them, since they may spray their surroundings.

Zorillas are solitary animals, coming together only to mate. The female is pregnant for about a month and gives birth in a burrow. Baby zorillas weigh only ½ ounce at birth, but they grow up fast. They begin eating solid food at about four and one-half weeks, but continue to nurse until they are eight weeks old.

Tree Porcupine
Coendou prehensilis

Length of the Body: 20 to 24 inches
Length of the Tail: about 16 inches
Diet: mainly leaves, fruits, and other plant matter

Number of Young: 1
Home: eastern South America
Weight: 9 to 13 pounds
Order: Rodents
Family: New World porcupines

 Rainforests

 Mammals

© JOHN SHAW / BRUCE COLEMAN INC.

Almost the entire body of the tree porcupine is covered with short spines. This large, stocky rodent relies on its spines for defense. The spines come off easily when the porcupine is attacked and embed themselves in the skin of the attacker. If a tree porcupine is caught out in the open, it rolls itself into a ball, exposing only its sharp spines.

Not surprisingly, the tree porcupine spends almost all of its time in trees and seldom visits the ground. Its long, spineless tail is prehensile, which means that it can be used like an extra hand to wrap around a branch. With its tail anchored to a branch, the porcupine can sleep, eat, move, or defend itself without fear of falling. Each foot has four toes with long, curved claws that help it hold onto branches and tree trunks.

Tree porcupines spend the day sleeping, either in a tree hole or hidden among dense foliage high above the ground. They look for food at night, slowly moving from one tree to another. They have poor eyesight, but excellent senses of smell, touch, and hearing.

At birth a baby tree porcupine weighs about 14 ounces. Its spines are soft, but they harden within a week. Like its parents, the baby has sharp claws on its toes. It can climb when it is only a few days old. Baby tree porcupines can be tamed. Some people in South America even keep them as pets.

Common Porpoise
Phocaena phocaena

Length: up to 6 feet
Weight: up to 120 pounds
Number of Young: 1
Home: north Pacific and north Atlantic Oceans

Diet: fish and squid
Order: Whales, dolphins, and porpoises
Family: Porpoises
Suborder: Toothed whales

 Oceans and Shores

 Mammals

© FLORIAN GRANER / NATURE PICTURE LIBRARY

Porpoises, like their relatives the dolphins and whales, are mammals that live in the sea. They are among the most intelligent animals in the world. Porpoises usually live in groups, playing and eating together. They nurse their young, as humans and other mammals do. They make their way in the water using a kind of sonar called echolocation and communicate with each other by clicking and whistling sounds.

Common porpoises are among the smaller kinds of porpoises. They may grow to a length of 6 feet and weigh 100 to 120 pounds. Their backs are black, and their undersides are white. Shaped like torpedoes,

they are very fast swimmers. The cool waters of the north Atlantic and north Pacific Oceans are home to the common porpoise. Sometimes these animals swim into harbors and even up rivers. For this reason, they are sometimes called harbor porpoises. Porpoises, like other mammals, have lungs, and they cannot stay underwater for very long without swimming to the surface for a breath of air.

Common porpoises usually mate during the summer. One young calf is born a year later. The female, or cow, nurses the calf with her milk for about a year. The male, or bull, does not help raise the calf.

Brush-tailed Possum
Trichosurus vulpecula

Length of the Body: 14 to 22 inches
Length of the Tail: 10 to 16 inches
Weight: 1 to 10 pounds (male); 3 to 8 pounds (female)

Diet: leaves, buds, and fruits
Number of Young: 1
Home: Australia, Tasmania, and New Zealand
Order: Marsupials
Family: Phalangers

 Forests and Mountains

 Mammals

© PAM GARDNER / FRANK LANE PICTURE AGENCY / CORBIS

The brush-tailed possum is one of the most common marsupial (pouched) mammals in Australia. It has long been hunted for its dense, woolly fur. Yet it continues to thrive. This creature is especially abundant in and around towns and farms. There, during the night, it often rustles through garbage and knocks over trash cans.

In 1940 these possums were introduced to New Zealand, where they quickly increased in number. They became pests because they damaged farmland and forest trees with their great appetite for leaves and tender buds. Brushtails eat a variety of vegetation, including eucalyptus and other plants poisonous to humans.

These possums sleep throughout the day. In the wild, they retire to tree hollows. Near cities and towns, they often sleep in attics. In yards, they sometimes seek shelter in bushes or abandoned rabbit burrows. Brushtails are solitary animals; only the female shares her nest—and only with her newborn.

Brush-tailed possums breed once or twice a year. Weighing barely a gram (or $\frac{3}{100}$ of an ounce), the newborn instinctively crawls from the birth canal into its mother's marsupial pouch. There it stays warm, nurses, and completes its development. The young brushtail becomes independent soon after leaving its mother's pouch.

Pygmy Flying Possum
Acrobates pygmaeus

Length of the Body: 2½ to 3¼ inches
Length of the Tail: 3 inches
Diet: nectar, tree sap, and insects

Number of Young: 3 or 4
Home: eastern Australia
Weight: ⅓ to ⅔ ounce
Order: Marsupials
Family: Pygmy phalangers

 Forests and Mountains

 Mammals

© B. G. THOMSON / PHOTO RESEARCHERS

The "flying possum" of Australia scampers along narrow tree branches and twigs. When it gets to the end of a branch, it launches itself into the air. It has a fold of skin on each side of its body that stretches from wrist to ankle. On these two "wings," it glides with limbs outstretched. Its strong, flexible tail works like a rudder.

This small rodent looks very much like a mouse. In fact, it is often referred to as a flying mouse. Some people call it the feathertail glider because of the feathery rows of hair on its tail. Since it is the smallest of the marsupial fliers, it is also known as the pygmy glider. Whatever the name, it is a tiny marsupial. All marsupials give birth to young that crawl into their mother's pouch and nurse until they are bigger.

The pygmy flying possum lives in the tallest trees in eucalyptus forests. It seldom, if ever, comes to the ground. During the day, this delicate little rodent sleeps in a nest about the size and shape of a baseball. It builds this home out of woven eucalyptus leaves, which it gathers under its curled tail. In the evening the possum leaves its nest to hunt insects, sip nectar, and eat blossoms.

The female pygmy possum gives birth to as many as four babies. Each weighs less than a gram, or .03 ounce, at birth. The young remain in their mother's pouch for two full months before venturing outside.

Common European Prawn (Palaemon)
Palaemon serratus

Length: up to 4⅓ inches
Number of Eggs: thousands
Home: eastern Atlantic Ocean,
    Black Sea, and
    Mediterranean Sea

Diet: smaller crustaceans,
    worms, and fish larvae
Order: Shrimps, crabs, and
    lobsters
Family: Palaemons

 Oceans and Shores

 Arthropods

© YVES LANCEAU / NHPA

The common European prawn, or palaemon, is well known in the fine restaurants of Europe and Japan. The most highly regarded of all European shrimp, it has a sweet, firm meat that fetches a high price. This shrimp is large enough to be marketed either whole or as tails.

Despite the name "common," this delicious creature is rare in the waters around Great Britain. It is a bit more common near rocks and seabeds in shallow coastal waters from Denmark south to Mauritania in West Africa. This species is closely related to the "common prawn" of North America, *Palaemonetus vulgaris*, a brown-spotted shrimp found along muddy shores from Massachusetts to Florida.

Like other palaemon shrimp, this species is equipped with small pincers on its front two pairs of legs. The shell, or carapace, extends over its head like a long, pointed snout. This extension is called a "rostrum." The rostrum of this prawn is especially long and armed with sawlike teeth.

Like most shrimp the common European prawn is social and swims in large schools near the seabed. It swims forward by paddling with its back legs and darts backward by snapping its tail. In spring and summer, the creatures swim to deep water to breed and lay eggs.

Pronghorn
Antilocapra americana

Length of the Body: up to 5 feet

Length of the Tail: 3 to 4 inches

Height at the Shoulder: up to 3½ feet

Weight: 84 to 90 pounds

Diet: herbs, leaves, and cacti

Number of Young: 1 to 3

Home: southern Saskatchewan south to Mexico

Order: Even-toed hoofed mammals

Family: Pronghorns

 Grasslands

 Mammals

Endangered Animals

The pronghorn is the fastest animal in the Western Hemisphere. In a burst of speed, it can reach 70 miles per hour. No natural predator—coyote, wolf, or cougar—can keep up.

In addition to speed, the pronghorn has keen eyesight and intelligence. On the open prairie, it can see a moving predator as far as 4 miles away. To warn its neighbors, a frightened pronghorn raises a patch of long white hairs on its rump. Other pronghorn can see this white "flag" for miles around. The pronghorn also releases a strong warning scent that even humans can smell.

While the pronghorn's speed and eyesight are great defenses against enemies, its intelligence almost brought disaster. These antelope are very inquisitive. When early American settlers arrived in the West, the pronghorn approached them out of curiosity. They were far too easy to slaughter. Many more pronghorn starved to death when ranchers began putting up fences. Since pronghorn refuse to jump over obstacles, they could not cross the prairie to reach their winter feeding grounds.

The good news is that the pronghorn is now on the increase across most of its range. Hunters are allowed to kill only a limited number each year. Still, two subspecies remain on the endangered list: the Sonoran pronghorn of Arizona and Mexico, and the peninsular pronghorn of Baja California.

Tufted Puffin
Lunda cirrhata

Length: about 15 inches
Weight: about 1¾ pounds
Diet: fish, squid, sea urchins, mollusks, and algae
Number of Eggs: 1

Home: northern Pacific Ocean
Order: Waders and gull-like birds
Family: Auks

 Oceans and Shores

  Birds

© BOB & CLARA CALHOUN / BRUCE COLEMAN INC.

The tufted puffin is the summertime clown of the north. During the summer breeding season, its face turns white, and its large bill becomes larger and reddish orange. At the same time, the bird grows long tufts of ivory-yellow head feathers, which droop over its ears and down the back of its neck. In winter the puffin loses these clownlike features.

Tufted puffins spend the winter far offshore in the cold, deep waters of the northern Pacific Ocean. There they use their excellent diving skills to pursue fish, squid, sea urchins, mollusks, and other underwater prey. In spring the puffins gather in large colonies on the steep cliffs of rocky islands and coastal slopes. After mating, the female lays a single blue egg in an underground burrow.

When the egg hatches, the parents take turns fetching fish and squid for their chick. They often carry several sea creatures at a time, crosswise in their large bill. The young puffins leave the nest when they are about 45 days old and spend the rest of the season learning to hunt with their parents.

Puffins, with their squat body and upright posture, look somewhat like penguins. However, these two types of birds are not closely related. They have come to resemble each other after ages of living in very similar, but widely separated, habitats.

Carpet Python
Morelia argus

Length: about 13 feet
Diet: small mammals and birds
Method of Reproduction: egg layer

Home: New Guinea and coastal Australia
Order: Lizards and snakes
Family: Pythons and boas

 Rainforests

 Reptiles

© STEVE COOPER / PHOTO RESEARCHERS

The markings of this Australian python reminded early settlers of the rich patterns in oriental carpets. And so the creature was named. The carpet python is found in various shades of brown with light-colored scales arranged in diamond-shaped designs. At 13 feet this python is among the giants of the snake world. Like other pythons, its body is stout and muscular. The scales on a python's back are smooth and tiny. Its belly scales, by contrast, are large and form plates across the bottom of the body. The python's head is small but far from harmless. Its mouth is filled with needle-sharp teeth.

Carpet pythons are most abundant in the jungle forests of New Guinea and northern Australia. They are equally at home in the treetops and on the ground. Sometimes the python hangs from a branch, then drops on an unsuspecting animal passing below. First the python snags its prey with its pointed teeth. Then it coils its body around its victim. As the python squeezes tighter and tighter, the captured bird or mammal has less and less room to breathe. Finally the prey suffocates and is swallowed whole.

The female carpet python broods her eggs by wrapping her body around them. Although she is cold-blooded, she can raise her body temperature by rhythmically contracting her muscles. In this way, she keeps her eggs warm during cool weather.

36

Green Tree Python
Chondropython viridis

Length: usually 3 to 4 feet
Diet: small mammals and birds
Home: New Guinea,
  northeastern Australia, and
  the Solomon and Aru islands

Method of Reproduction: egg
  layer
Order: Lizards and snakes
Family: Pythons and boas

 Rainforests

 Reptiles

© JOE MCDONALD / CORBIS

The green tree python is completely at home at the top of the rainforest. Nearly invisible among the vines and leaves, the snake anchors itself to a branch with its strong, flexible tail. From this secure perch, the python waits to strike its prey. Birds, bats, and rodents are among its many victims. After grabbing hold with its long front teeth, the green python wraps its body around the prey and squeezes. The snake swallows the suffocated victim whole.

After laying her eggs, the female green python wraps herself around them, providing warmth and protection. Her newborns are usually lemon-yellow, with spots of purple and brown. As they mature, all the young snakes turn leaf green. The adult green python has a broken stripe of white or dull yellow down its back.

The green tree python looks virtually identical to the emerald tree boa of the South American rainforest. Living a world apart, the two species are only distantly related. That they look so similar is an example of "parallel evolution." Parallel evolution takes place when two separate species evolve to live nearly identical lifestyles in very similar environments. Both green pythons and emerald boas are fast hunters that race through the jungle treetops with near-invisible grace. One great difference between the two species: the emerald boa gives birth to live babies, while the green python lays eggs.

37

Reticulate Python
Python reticulatus

Diet: birds and mammals, including poultry, cats, and dogs
Method of Reproduction: egg layer

Home: Southeast Asia
Length: up to 33 feet
Order: Lizards and snakes
Family: Boas

 Rainforests

 Reptiles

© JOE MCDONALD / CORBIS

Reticulate pythons live in jungles, climbing from branch to branch in search of prey. These huge reptiles even live near towns and farms, hiding during the day and hunting at night. Many islands in Southeast Asia are now inhabited by these creatures, because the pythons are good swimmers that will even swim in ocean waters.

A reticulate python is easy to spot. Putting aside its enormous length (up to 33 feet, making it the largest python in the world), you can recognize this snake by its small eyes and small nostrils. Under the nostrils are two grooves filled with organs that sense differences in temperature. These organs help the python find birds, mammals, and other prey because they sense the difference in temperature between the prey's body and the surrounding air.

Once a reticulate python has sensed a nearby victim, the snake silently waits for it to come near. Then, in a lightning-fast motion, the python shoots out from its hiding place and grabs the prey with its jaws. A python kills its victim by constriction. That is, it wraps itself around the prey's body and squeezes until the prey can no longer breathe. The prey dies from suffocation, and the python eats it whole!

A female reticulate python lays up to 100 eggs, each the size of a tennis ball. She pushes the eggs into a pile and coils herself around them, incubating the eggs for two to three months, until they hatch.

Rock Python
Python sebae

Diet: rodents, birds, and small mammals
Method of Reproduction: egg layer

Home: Africa
Length: up to 25 feet
Order: Scaly reptiles
Family: Pythons and boas

 Grasslands

Reptiles

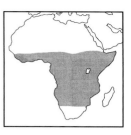

© JOE MCDONALD / CORBIS

The rock python spends its life slithering through the grass in the savannas of Africa. This reptile is easy to recognize—a dark arrowhead-shaped mark dominates the top of its head. It is classified as a "primitive snake" because it still retains small hip and leg bones inside of its body. These now-useless bones are left over from a time, millions of years ago, when snakes evolved from lizards.

The pythons are among the longest land animals in Africa and are certainly some of the largest snakes on Earth. The rock python hunts at night using heat-sensitive organs near its mouth to find warm-blooded prey. When it catches an animal in its jaws, the rock python wraps its long, powerful body around the prey and squeezes it to death. Then the snake secretes large amounts of saliva to help slide the prey down its throat. The python will attack surprisingly large animals, swallowing them whole. A 13-foot-long python was once found with a 60 pound antelope in its stomach!

Despite its size and ferocious appetite, the rock python seldom threatens humans; when approached, the snake usually slithers away. However, the experts agree, it is best to avoid any python right after it has captured its prey. A python jealously guarding a meal will turn and strike with its enormous mouth wide open.

Little Button Quail
Turnix sylvatica

Length: about 6 inches
Weight: about 1½ ounces
Diet: plants, seeds, and insects
Number of Eggs: usually 4

Home: southern Portugal and Spain, Africa, and southern Asia
Order: Cranes and rails
Family: Button quails

 Grasslands

 Birds

© ROLAND SEITRE / PETER ARNOLD, INC.

Although they greatly resemble true quail, little button quail are more closely related to long-legged cranes. Round as buttons, these shy birds spend most of their lives hidden in low bushes and thick grasses. They grow plump on a diet of grass seeds and plant shoots; they also catch insects and spiders.

The female button quail is larger, feistier, and more brightly colored than her mate. She takes the lead during courtship, displaying her feathers and calling with a low, booming voice. In their competition for males, female button quail frequently battle among themselves. In Asia the quarrelsome females are often captured and cruelly forced to fight for the amusement of onlookers.

The female button quail lays her clutch of eggs in a simple nest scratched among grass or beneath low bushes. She then leaves her mate to tend the nest and raise their young. Some females lay several clutches of eggs, leaving each one in the care of a different male.

The eggs take only 13 days to hatch, one of the shortest incubation times for any bird. Soon after they are born, the chicks hop from their nest and follow their father. They begin to flutter when they are just a week old and can fly in about two weeks. At that point the young button quail can survive on their own. But their father usually keeps the family together for nearly a month.

Quetzal
Pharomachrus mocino

Length of the Body: 11 to 12 inches
Length of the Tail: up to 3 feet
Weight: about 7 ounces
Diet: fruits and insects

Number of Eggs: usually 2
Home: Mexico and Central America
Order: Trogons
Family: Trogons

 Rainforests

 Birds

© KEVIN SCHAFER / PETER ARNOLD, INC.

? Endangered Animals

Each year the male quetzal grows a magnificent train of green feathers on top of its true tail. During the mating season, females generally mate with the male who has the longest, most attractive plumes. The beauty and length (sometimes almost 3 feet) of these feathers, or "coverts," earned the quetzal sacred status among the Aztecs and Mayans. In centuries past, these ancient peoples ventured into the bird's mountainous jungle home in search of plumes to use for ceremonial purposes.

Despite its elaborate train, the male shares in the incubation of the eggs. Since the quetzal's nest is usually built in a tree hole, the male has an awkward time climbing in, and must, in fact, drape its fantastic plumage outside the hole. Predators, poachers, and feather collectors needn't look far to find some plumes for the picking. After a few days of nest sitting, the long feathers become battered and broken and eventually fall to the ground, to be regrown the following year.

Even without his tail feathers, the male quetzal is a striking bird, with a ruby breast and tufts of green feathers on his head and back. The female has duller colors and a much shorter tail. This bird is endangered, both from poachers and from the continuing destruction of its rainforest home—the mountainous jungles of Mexico and Central America.

European Wild Rabbit
Oryctolagus cuniculus

Length: 15 to 20 inches
Diet: grasses and other plant matter
Number of Young: usually 4 to 6

Weight: 2 to 4 pounds
Home: native to Europe; introduced elsewhere
Order: Lagomorphs
Family: Rabbits and hares

 Grasslands

 Mammals

© TONY HAMBLIN / FRANK LANE PICTURE AGENCY / CORBIS

The European wild rabbit is a social animal that lives in colonies in underground burrows called warrens. During the day the rabbit stays underground or in other hiding places. But at dusk and during the night, it emerges to feed on grass, clover, and other tender plants. European wild rabbits have large front teeth, called incisors, that grow throughout the animal's lifetime. The incisors are the rabbit's main tool when it comes time to nibble on the plants that are its food.

Europeans introduced this species to Australia, New Zealand, and other places. The rabbits had no natural enemies in these new homes, so their populations grew rapidly. The rabbits caused widespread damage, both to crops and to native plants. In Australia, these animals even compete with sheep and cattle for food. The European wild rabbit is also the ancestor of common tame (domesticated) rabbits.

Rabbit populations can increase quickly because rabbits reproduce frequently. A female may produce three or four litters a year, each with as many as 12 babies. The young are born in an underground burrow that the mother has lined with straw and fur. They are born without hair and with their eyes closed, and weigh less than 2 ounces. They grow rapidly; and by the time a European wild rabbit is about six months old, it can begin to reproduce.

Dark-green Racer
Coluber viridiflavus

Diet: mainly lizards; also small rodents, frogs, and insects
Method of Reproduction: egg layer

Home: Western Europe
Length: 5 to 6½ feet
Order: Lizards and snakes
Family: Colubrid snakes

 Forests and Mountains

Reptiles

© DANIEL HEUCLIN / NHPA

The dark-green racer "races" over the ground, reaching truly great speeds for a snake, especially when disturbed or chasing a particularly tasty morsel. Despite its speed, the dark-green racer is not easy to spot. Its upper side is dark, blending in with its surroundings. Its lower side is light. The racer is a fairly slender snake, with a long, thin tail and a sharp ridge of scales above each eye.

The dark-green racer lives in rocky and very mountainous areas of Western Europe. In the Pyrenees and Alps, it is found as high as 4,500 feet above sea level. There the reptile basks in a sunny spot surrounded by bushes and other low plant growth. In many parts of southwestern Europe, the dark-green racer is a common sight near stone walls.

Although these snakes spend most of their time on the ground, they are good swimmers and climbers, often slithering up bushes to raid bird nests. They grab and swallow small prey live. Larger prey is first killed by constriction, then swallowed whole. The dark-green racer is not poisonous, but if it is bothered, it may inflict a painful bite.

Racers, like other snakes, do not hear most sounds that travel through the air. Instead, they sense vibrations through the ground. These vibrations tell the racers of approaching predators and other changes in the environment.

Pod Razor
Ensis siliqua

Length: up to 8 inches
Width: up to 1⅓ inches
Diet: plankton
Home: northeastern Atlantic Ocean and the Mediterranean Sea

Method of Reproduction: egg layer
Order: Quahogs, razor clams, and their relatives
Family: Razor clams

 Oceans and Shores

Other Invertebrates

© LAURIE CAMPBELL / NHPA

Along the shores of Great Britain and the Mediterranean Sea, beachcombers harvest pod razors at low tide. It's easy to get at the clam's tasty meat by breaking its brittle shell. Razor clams (there are several species) are all named for their long, narrow shell. The pod razor, for instance, is six times longer than it is wide. This gives the clam the shape of an old-fashioned straight-edged shaving razor.

The pod razor's long, narrow shape enables it to quickly burrow into the mud to hide from its enemies. The shell has a special hole through which the clam extends a long, muscular foot. The clam stretches its foot down into the mud and then retracts it. In this way, it pulls the rest of its body underground. The clam pushes and pulls its foot and shell until it is deeply buried.

The pod razor cannot eat when it is buried. Its siphon, the tube through which it feeds, is too short. So the clam must pop back to the surface when it is hungry. Like most clams, pod razors catch food by sucking water into their siphon. From the water, they filter tiny, floating plants and animals called plankton.

When the pod razor is alive and wet, its shell is covered by a dark green or yellowish-green skin. Empty pod razor shells lose their living skin and so look creamy white, often with reddish-brown streaks or blotches.

Set Index